P9-CQW-542

W/8/15

16251 on circle.

Silent Night is a WALTZ!

5 operations for majors

R C G C
D C G B

C

F# G

F C# D

Also play ... I II III II I

F C G# A

C G D# E

C△7 Dm7 | Em7 Am | C△7

Printed on 100% recycled paper.

I GOT RHYTHM CHANGES

$I_{\triangle 7}$	VI_{m7}	II_{m7}	V_7
(Chord) $C_{\triangle 7}$	Am_7	Dm_7	G_7 ①⑥②⑤ of C
$B\flat$ $F_{\triangle 7}$	Dm_7	Gm_7	C_7 of F
$BE\flat$ $B\flat$	Gm_7	Cm_7	F_7
$BEA\flat$ $E\flat_{\triangle}$	Cm_7	F_7	$B\flat$
$BEAD\flat$ $A\flat_{\triangle}$	F_7	$B\flat$	$E\flat_{\triangle}$
$BEADG\flat$ $D\flat_{\triangle}$	$D\flat$	$E\flat$	$A\flat$
$F\sharp$ $G\sharp$	$D_{\triangle}$	$A_{\triangle}$	$D_{\triangle}$

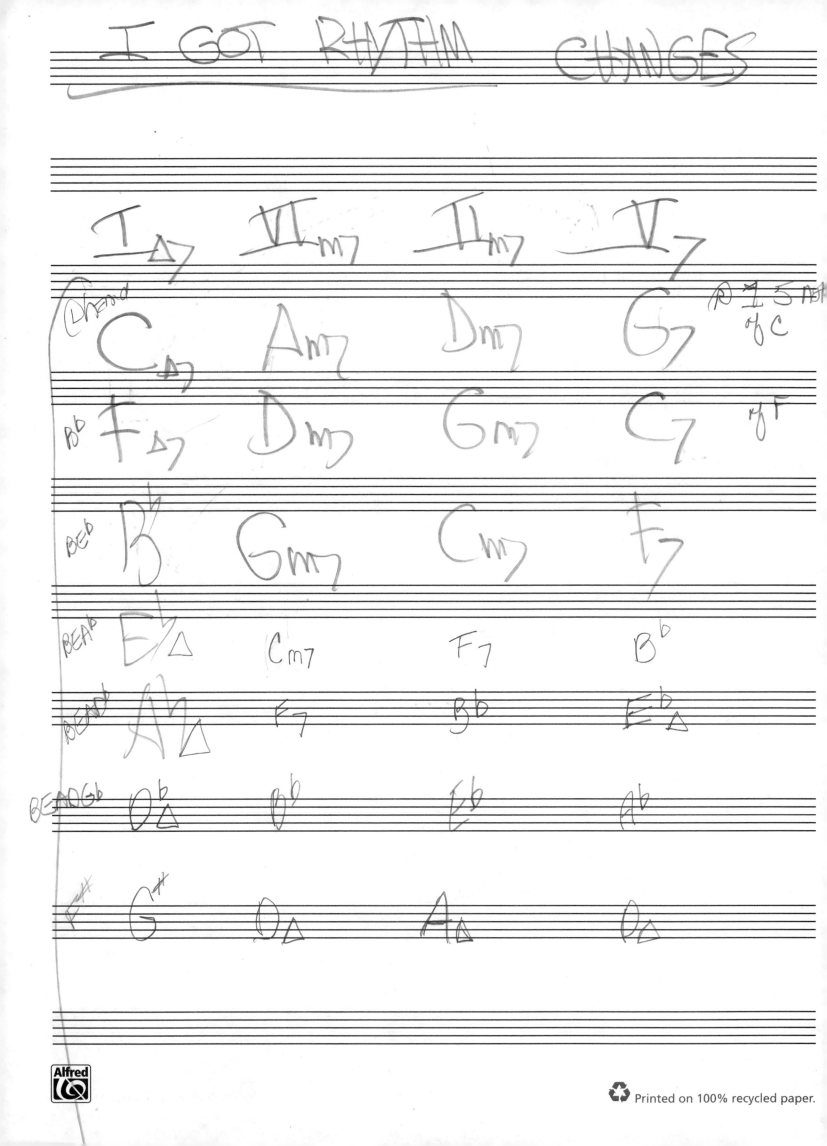

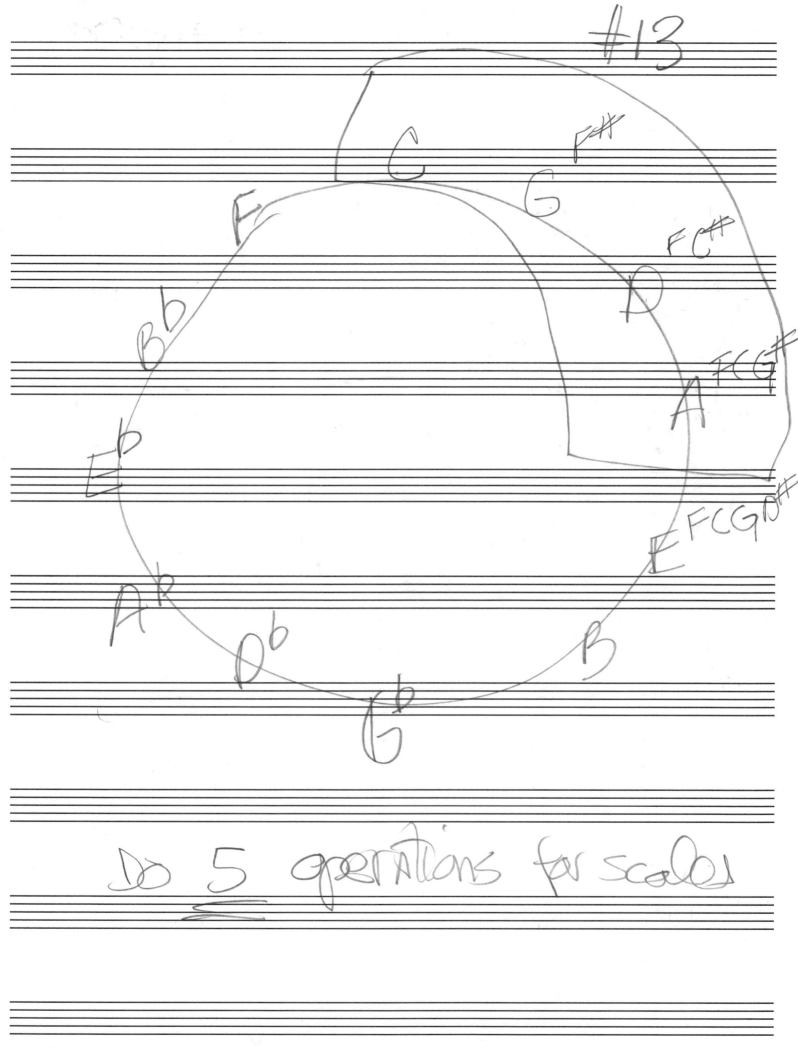

Do 5 operations for scales

HANNON - start on #38

(symetry) (Reverse symetry)
(contrary motion) (parallel motion)

3 things to be AWARE of...

1) step / leap

2) Ascending / descending

3) trill (neighbor notes) 3 notes

look at 1st bar, ~~Ascending~~ descending

Printed on 100% recycled paper.

4 types of movement
of 2 voices/notes

1) parallel

2) contrary

3) similar

4) oblique

@ hand until #5²

continue "5 operations for
major scales"

"shell concept
cookie cutter"

MASTER
SONG LIST

1) SILENT / C / WALTZ   p. 16 Blue Book

2) BEAUTY / C / STRAIGHT

3) Can't Help falling in Love / C /   p. 28 Blue Book
4) Try to Remember / C /   p. 138 Blue Book

#15

play waltz
groove around clock
and
chromatically

I   V

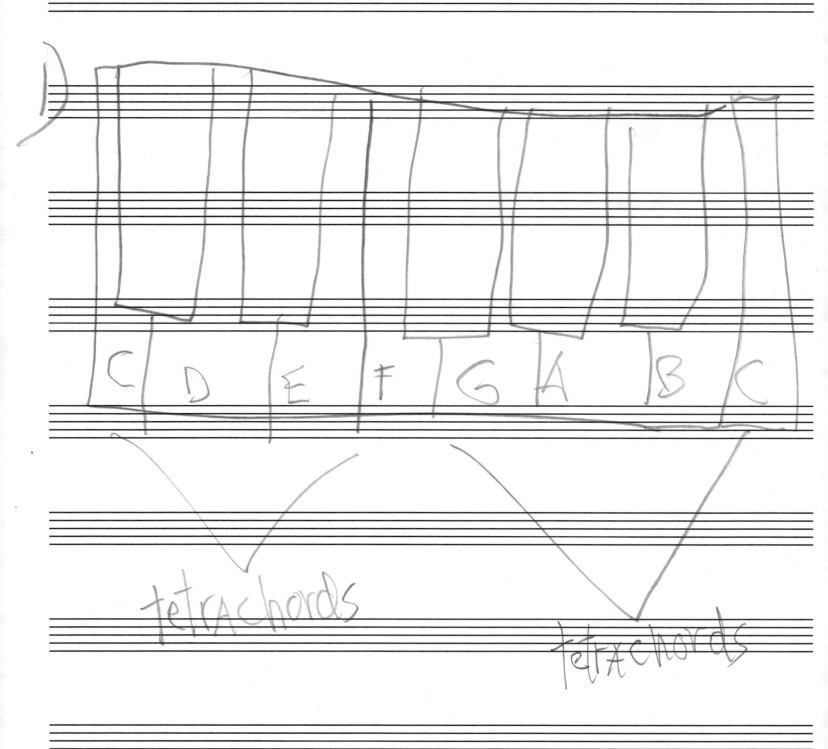

tetrachords

tetrachords

11-12-18

Hanon #39 A minor x2

Chapel
Authoritone
1st Fri
1015AM

Fur Elise p. 77 (A) (B) section

11-20-18 1st 3 pages of Music Math Drill

Hanon   A Minor
~~F Major~~
~~D Major~~   melodic minor

p. 50
#38   Fur Elise p. 76
              Music by Masters

A minor + E major   memorize 1st section
    i   V   B   of Fur Elise
         E
      E
   R
   B   R

                    Root, 3rd, 5th

Am   E
8   #8
I   IV
C   G
          8
8

Printed on 100% recycled paper.

Alfred

 Alfred

♻ Printed on 100% recycled paper.

Printed on 100% recycled paper.

Printed on 100% recycled paper.